Antigua and Barbuda

Antigua and Barbuda Dictionary

is a collection of expressive words and phrases

Jerene Joseph

Antigua and Barbuda Dictionary

Antigua and Barbuda Dictionary

Table of **Content**

Acknowledgement	5
Introduction	6
A	8-9
B	10-16
C	16-22
D	22-26
E	26
F	26-30
G	30-32
H	32-34
I	34-35
J	35-37
K	38-39
L	39-42
M	42-45
N	45-46
O	46-47
P	47-51
Q	51-52
R	52-54
S	54-60
T	60-63
U	63
V	63-64
W	64-67
Y	67
Z	67-68
Expression and sayings	69-75
References	77

Antigua and Barbuda Dictionary

Acknowledgement

This dictionary would not have been possible without the support and assistance from my sister, Terry Joseph-Simon and my brother, Gabby Joseph. Much thanks to them for their contribution.

Copyright @ 2019

Jerene Joseph

Introduction

The Antigua and Barbuda dictionary is a collection of expressive words and phrases.

Antigua and Barbuda consists of two inhabited islands and is located between the Caribbean Sea and Atlantic Ocean. English is the official language but many of the island residents speak an English-based Creole. The use of Creole on the island varies depending on socioeconomic class. Speakers from lower social standing tends to speak Creole more readily since they more likely to have left school early. Broadly speaking, as one moves up on the social class scale due to education, occupation, and income they tend to use more features belonging to standard English but can effortlessly shift between standard English and their local Creole dialect. In Antigua and Barbuda, the use of creole is more common and less alike to standard English.

The creole spoken in Antigua and Barbuda as well as other English-speaking Caribbean islands derived from slaves blending English and other West African languages during slavery. Enslaved people who were brought to the Caribbean from different West African regions spoke a variety of languages. Consequently, the language imposed upon them by their white colonial plantation oppressors was English. By mixing their West African language and English, they created what is known as Antigua and Barbuda Creole.

Antigua and Barbuda Dictionary

A

a'aye	an idiomatic expression - used *to* acknowledge or communicate something
abay	to taunt by sticking out the tongue
aboo	a chalk like stone that is used for writing on a slate (handheld chalkboard)
acardin	according
achar	a condiment made with mango, vinegar, salt, pepper, and mustard seed
actoba	October
advantage tekka	a person who takes advantage of another person
afta/atta	after
ah chue	it's true
ah deh ee deh	there it is
ah fu me	it's my own
ah fu yu	it's yours
ah good	that's good for you; serves you right
ah nah chue	it's not true
ah nah fu me	it's not mine
ah nah so	it's not so
ah wah do?	How are you?
ah way ee deh	Where is it?
ah way yu ah go?	Where are you going?
all fools' day	known as a day for practical jokes and pranks
all fours	an English tavern trick taking two players card game and can be played

Antigua and Barbuda Dictionary

	as a four players game with variations to its standard rules
ana	not
anchoba	eggplant
ansa	answer
antie man	a homosexual male
antiga	Antigua
apple banana	baby banana; finger rows
arda	order
argas	August
aright	alright
arl	all
arm hole	armpit; an opening for the arm in a garment
arnda	under
arwe	us; we
aryu	you all
ashum	roasted grind corn with sugar
ass	ask
assue/box	a form of savings where a group of people pay an agreed sum of money on a periodic basis (usually monthly) and each period one member of the group takes all the money that have been paid
attanoon	afternoon
avispa	wasp
ayodeze	second person plural pronoun; you plural
ayulard	an expression of shock and disgust

B

babash	a potent over proof rum with a fearsome reputation
babylon	an oppressive or corrupt system or regime. The United States of America
bacchanal	a carnival; large party; celebration; scandal; conflict or drama
back a day	previously; in the past
back chat	the act of talking or replaying back to a parent or someone in authority
back hand	to strike or slap someone using the back part of the hand
back stabber	a person who betrays another
backa	in the back of
back-back	to reverse; to move backwards
backside	an expression used to convey excitement or disbelief
bad feeling	a feeling of sickness in the stomach; nausea; morning sickness
bad gait	bad habit
bad john	a bully or gangster
bad minded	refer to a person who is jealous and envious
bad tark	to criticize or to say unkind things about a person
badda	to worry or to be bothersome
baddaration	to pester someone; to be bothersome

Antigua and Barbuda Dictionary

badwodd	curse words or expression for curse words
bafany	one who is disabled or have a physical abnormality
baide	to take a bath or shower
bagsaroocoo	a person who is very dark in complexion
bag twine	the string from a crocus or flour bag
bake	a firm round bread - can be baked or fried
bakkle	bottle
bakkra	white slave owner or master
baku	ghost or spirit of a dead person
bamboola	a round flat bread made from grated cassava
bang dawg	an abundant supply of something
bang up	to beat up or to assault
bang	to beat
bangles	bracelets
bankin	elevated rows of soil where vegetables are planted
barefaced	the act of not trying to hide one's bad behavior or manners
barra	to borrow
bart	a large round aluminum tub used for bathing or washing clothes
bassa bassa	fooling around
bassman	an informal title used for greeting among male friends

Antigua and Barbuda Dictionary

bata bata	a heavy load that impede a person progress that causes them to move slowly
bath suit	swim suit/bathing suit
batten dung	a fruit tree that is laden with fruits; to secure a home by closing all windows and doors
battom foot	the sole of the feet
battum	bottom; rear end
batty bwoy	a homosexual male
batty hole	anus
batty	buttocks or rear end
bawl plenty	to cry or weep for a long time
bawl	to cry; to shout on someone
bawn	born
bax dung	to hit or strike with an open palm slap
bax	box; to hit
bay	beach
baybee	baby
bayka	baker
bayside	seaside or beach
bedden	old clothing that's used as linen to sleep on at night
before time	long time ago
behine	behind; buttocks or rear end
belly cutting	belly ache; upset stomach
belly swell bakkle	a bottle that contains a dark liquid and is tied to the branch of a fruit tree to deter potential thieves.

Antigua and Barbuda Dictionary

	There is a belief that if the fruit is eaten by anyone their stomach would become swollen.
benna	a type of two or three-line folk song repeated over and over
berring grung	burial ground; cemetery; graveyard
bess	best
betta	better
bex	to be angry or upset
big toan	swollen testicle
big up	to make a shout out to someone
bill	a hand-held tool used for cutting hard objects such as coconut or wood
bine up	to be constipated
birdspeed	to move very fast
birth paper	birth certificate
bitter bush	a vine bearing a small bumpy skinned yellow or orange fruit. The leaves are used to make a bitter herbal tea
blabba mouth	a person who talks a lot and unable to keep information confidential
black ile	a black sticky substance that is used especially for road surfaces
black led	pencil
blank	to ignore
blasted	used to express annoyance
blaze	to hit hard
blows	to hit repeatedly

Antigua and Barbuda Dictionary

bludda	a balloon
blue Tuesday	after a public holiday on Monday people take off the Tuesday
bobolee	an idiot; a stupid or gullible person
bogoment	the burro banana is square in shape and when ripened the banana flavor is creamy and sweet with a lemon flavor undertone
boldface	one who is brazen
bombs	fire cracker
bonnet	the hood of a vehicle
bony	skinny
boobie	pelican
bore	to make holes through the ear lobes with a needle or needle gun
bout	about
bragadang	idiomatic expression - the sound made by a person when a large object falls
brap/bradam	a sudden stop
brawta	bonus or extra add on to something being purchased from a seller
bread & cheese tree	a wild shrub that is used as fencing and the soft flesh attached to the seed can be eaten
bread pet	the soft inside of the bread
bread plat	a long thin twisted piece of dough that is placed on top of a loaf of bread before baking
brebbish	a mixture of water and sugar

breed off	to impregnate; the act taken to become pregnant
breed	to become pregnant or a woman who is frequently pregnant
breeding-bag	placenta or afterbirth
breeze off	to take a rest
breeze	washing powder
brisk	to be nosy or showing excessive curiosity about the affairs of others
brodda	brother
broughtupsy	proper upbringing or home training
bruck	to be out of money; to break something
bruck way	to break away
buba	clothes
bubble	to gyrate or bounce one's rear end up and down to the beat of music
bubby kipupah	bra/brazier
bubby	breast
bud	penis
buhbul	an act that is meant to be deceitful
bulf	bulb
bull bud	a whip made from a stretched-out sun dried cow penis and is used as a weapon
bull poop	a male who engages in anal sex
bull work	hard physical work
bull	to have sexual intercourse
bulla	a homosexual male
bully beef	canned corned beef

bumpa	buttocks or rear end
bun	burn; a sweet round bread with raisins
bun me	to dislike the action of another person
bun tart	a sweet pastry with coconut filling
bush tea	leaves taken from specific tropical fruit trees (i.e. lime, sugar apple, soursop) to make hot tea. Bush tea is a Caribbean parents remedy for treating most physical ailments
buss	burst; bus
busta	a hard-chewy dark brown candy made from sugar, coconut, and ginger
butt up pan	to meet by accident
butt	to be gored by a cow; sugar cane that is cut into pieces at the blade joint
bwile	boil
bwoy	a boy or young male

C

cacanafoon	to tumble
cackle water	a stew made with clams or cockles
cakkle	cattle
cakkle bwile	a sty or an infection of the eyelid resulting from a blocked oil gland

Antigua and Barbuda Dictionary

calabash	a large inedible gourd. The gourd when dried can be used as a bowl
calypso	a genre of Afro-Caribbean music that originated in Trinidad and Tobago
calypsonian	one who sings songs of the calypso genre
cambo	scars or marks on the arms or legs
campha ball	moth balls
can cup	a cup made from enamel
cane peel	the outer covering of the sugar cane
cane tap	the long leaf of the sugar cane plant
canfusion	confusion
cappa	one cent
cark up	to be constipated
carkings	a dodged ball game
carn	corn; can't
carna	corner
carna yai	to look or gaze at someone from the corners of the eye
cassie	edible cactus leaves or nopal
cata nine	multiple whips woven together
catapult	a sling shot made from a forked stick with elastic band fastened to the two prongs
catta	a wad of cloth or cushion that's placed on the head to facilitate the carrying of a heavy load
cawz	cause
chackter	tractor

chap chap/chap up	cooked okra, spinach, papaya or eggplant that's mashed and sometimes blended together
chap	to cut
charklit	roasted whole cocoa beans grounded and used for making cocoa tea
chat	to talk
chatta box	a person who talks a lot or too much
ched	copulation of a rooster and hen
cheese and bread	wow; goodness!
chickie wig	young green tamarind
chiclet panty	none cotton underwear
chigga	trigger; hives
chimb	a moderate haircut
chimble	tremble; shiver
ching gum	chewing gum
chinnydad	Trinidad
chips	french fries
cho	a word used to express pleasant surprise
choba	eggplant
chook	to stab or poke
choway	to throw away; to abort a pregnancy
chrison	a religious blessing of a baby
Christmas bush	the leaves and tree of Pimenta racemosa; used culinarily and to produce the cologne called bay rum
chub fish	parrot fish

Antigua and Barbuda Dictionary

chubble	trouble
chuch	church
chuck	to shove or push
chucoo chucoo	failure to thoroughly complete a task
chue	true
chuesday	Tuesday
chula	an outside wood burning oven constructed of dirt, stones or bricks
chune up	the act of provoking or inciting a person to act out verbally or physically
chune	tune
chupit	stupid
chupitness	to talk nonsense
chups	the sucking of one's teeth to express disagreement - can be said or done
church bread	a thin piece of unleavened bread used during Holy Communion
cistern	a concrete structure built under a brick house foundation for collecting and storing rain water
claffy	an idiot or stupid person
clammy	sticky
clamon cherry	a sticky fruit like berry that is light pale to brown or even pink in color. The pulp in a ripe berry can be used as an alternative to paper glue
clappas	mouth
claps	venereal disease

Antigua and Barbuda Dictionary

clart	cloth or fabric
clati	an exaggerated expression used to identify the intensity of a strike
clear skin	a light or fair skinned person but not a white person
cloze	closed; clothes
coal kill	a pit that is dug in the ground where wood is placed to burn and eventually turn into coal.
coal pot	a cooking device using wood or charcoal, consisting of a raised iron or clay bowl and a central grid
cock battum	a person who has a high protruding rear end
cockeye	crossed eye
cock up	to bend over and extend ones' buttocks in the air; to sit in a vulgar manner
cockle	edible marine mollusk
cocobay	leprosy
coconut broom	a yard broom made from the dried spines of the coconut branch
coconut drops	a round pastry made from grated coconut, sugar, flour, raisins, spices and other ingredients
coconut jelly	the soft flesh of a young coconut
coconut wharf	a coconut grove or plantation
coffee woman	a fortune teller
cog	to cheat or to copy from another student class work

Antigua and Barbuda Dictionary

colic	upset stomach
com back yah	come back here
com yah	come here
common soap	an everyday all-purpose soap
confine	to give birth; to have a baby
confirmation	rites of passage practice by Christian denominations
congo	eel; french braid
contree	country; country side
cookahole	anus
cook up	a one pot dish
cooka	to defecate; rear end
coocumba	cucumber
coolie hair	straight hair
coolie	a person of East Indian ancestry
cool-out	take it easy; to relax
coop	to spy on; to be sneaky
coruckles	mess; junk
couda	could have
cowich	an itchy fibrous material used in wall insulation
cowl	cold
crall	crawl
crappo foot	handwriting that is not legible
crappo	frog or toad
crarp	to scratch
crass	a vicious dog
crazy house	an institution where people with mental illness are kept and treated
crocus bag	a large brown woven sack

cross and north	tic-tac-toe
cruffy	rough dry skin
cry wata	tears
cu pan yu	look at you
cu yah	look here
cuff	to strike across the head
cum cum saw	just come; thinks he knows it all
cunks/conch	a sea-dwelling mollusk or large-oversize snail. It's considered a delicacy
cunumunu	a stupid person; a man who is easily controlled by a woman
cupadip	poison
currant	electricity
cuss	curse
cut style	failure to engage or to show interest
cutex	nail polish
cut-eye	a visual gesture using the eyes and face to communicate displeasure
cutlyss	a large flat bladed knife
cyaan	cannot

D

dagga	a short knife or stick with a sharp pointed edge
daggarin	a type of dance that incorporate sexual movements or gestures
dagger tree	a tropical plant with sword-like foliage that originate from the center of the plant.

Antigua and Barbuda Dictionary

dall-up	to dress up; to beautify oneself
dam nasty	very nasty
dandan	a pretty dress
dandy ball	bubble gum or gumball
darb	to rub or to spread
darlie playthings	doll accessories
darlie	doll
darre	expensive
darta	daughter
dasheen	a tropical plant (taro) grown primarily for its edible root and leaves
dashway	to throw away; to discard; to abort a pregnancy
dat deh	that there
dat	that
dawg	dog
daywid	to be involve in a relationship
de	the
dead house	the morgue
deblish	a term used to describe a person who is a trouble maker or a bully
deesant	decent
deh	there
dem	them – third person plural
dif	deaf
dilly	sapodilla - an oval, ellipsoidal or conical fruit varying in size from 2 to 4 inches in width
dinna	dinner

dipeen	to enter a conversation, argument or quarrel
dis yah	this here
disgustin	a person who is troublesome or bothersome
do arf	to have sexual intercourse
doctor bird	humming bird
doe	door
dokosay	a short person
donkey feeder	a straw hat
doog doog	a small plastic bottle used for carrying water
door mouth	doorway or door entrance
dortish	dumb, stupid
double up	a soup like stew make from a variety of vegetables and meats
douve dung	meat, fish or chicken that is fried then stewed
draff	draft
drap wodd	comments made that is directed or intended for someone in your presence
drap	an animal that gave birth; to drop an object
draw	to strike or to light a match
drawz	men and women underwear
dread nut	coconut
dressing table	dresser; vanity
dribble	drool
dribe	drive

Antigua and Barbuda Dictionary

drop sleep	to fall asleep
drop the ball	to be replaced
drum	a cylindrical container used for collecting and storing water
drunkard	an alcoholic
ducana	a dish made from grated sweet potato, grated coconut, flour, sugar and other spices. The mixture is blend together and wrapped in foil, grape or banana leaf then boiled in water until firm
duldul night	an annual event that once took place on November 5th characterized by bonfire and fireworks. The purpose was for people to burn their bad memories.
dumar	a person who is very dark skinned and hard to see at night
dums	a small round berry. The fruit is green and turns yellow as it ripens (jujube)
dun	done
dunce bright	a person who is not as smart as he or she believes
dunce	one who is a slow learner; a stupid person
dung day	down there
dung gut	a person with a large distended abdomen
dung	down

dunkaydam	indifferent
duppy	spirit or ghost of a dead person
dutty gyal	a very sweet dark brown coconut sugar cake
dutty whine	a dance that involve coordinated movement of the hips, knees, and head
dutty	dirty or unclean

E

e'bang good	it tastes good
ease up	to lighten up; to forgive
eba	ever
ebery	every
eberyting	everything
edday tap	edible leaves of the taro corm
edge	teeth sensitivity to cold or sweets
edge-up	to kiss up or to mingle with people outside of one's social class
eedyat	idiot
eef	if; to agree with someone
ent' it	isn't it
ettie	a ripe fruit that looks pretty
expeck	expect
ezee	a person who is easy going

F

face basin	an enamel wash-basin for washing the face and hands

fada giver	one who gives the bride away
falla fashing	to imitate; copycat
falla	to follow
fallout	to stop speaking; to terminate a relationship or friendship after a disagreement
fanner	a portable handheld fan
fantail	a bridal veil
farda	father
farden	a former British monetary unit equal to ¼ of a penny
fark	fork
farmfool	to behave foolishly
farrid	forehead
fars	a nosey or inquisitive person
fart	to be afraid; frightened; to pass gas
farwodd	to be rude and insulting
fayva	favor
fed up	the state of being frustrated with someone, something, or a situation
fedda	feather
feel up	to test the firmness of a fruit by squeezing; to fondle by squeezing and caressing the body
fete	a party or celebration
fever grass	a topical plant in the grass family cultivated as a medicinal herb (lemon grass)
fig	banana

Antigua and Barbuda Dictionary

finga rows	the smallest of the banana varieties (apple banana)
fish pot	traps used for catching fish
fits	seizure
flambeau	a flare torch – usually a bottle with kerosene and a piece of cloth
flit can	an elongated canister used for spraying insects
flit	to spray
flittaz	fritters
florie tambran	a tamarind that is half green and half ripe
flowaz	flowers
fluxie	a fruit that is not fully matured
flym	film
flyshit face	freckles
follow	to accompany; to mix with people of bad reputation
fool arf	to be dishonest
fooly	a stupid person
force ripe	a young child acting like a grown up; a fruit that is forced to ripened prematurely
form	grade levels
forrin	foreign; to immigrate to countries familiarly known; the United States of America
four-day marnin	early morning
frack	dress

Antigua and Barbuda Dictionary

fraico	a sweet treat made with shaved ice and topped with flavored fruit syrup
fraid	to be afraid
fraidukin	a person who is afraid of a physical confrontation
fram	from
frawth	to speak or to write nonsense
freebs	things that are free
fresh	a man or women who talks provocatively or make sexual advances towards a person of the opposite sex
freshwater yankee	someone who visited America for a short period and return to their home in the Caribbean with an American dialect
fret up	to worry
fretting	to argue or to fuss
frig up	a person who gets annoyed easily
frig	synonym for fuck
friken	to be frightened, scared, or overly excited
front end lifter	beverages made from herbs or roots and intended to strengthen the back and improve sexual performance
frouzy	having a strong-smelling body odor
frozen joy	frozen popsicle treats made from pureed tropical fruits or custard
fruzie	molasses

fry dumplin	a dough made with flour, salt, butter, baking powder, water and sometimes sugar. The dough is formed into multiple round balls, flattened, and fry in oil.
fu chue	it's true
fu he	it's his
fu me	it's mine
fu she	it's hers
fu yu	it's yours
fujou	cool
full	when a fruit is mature and ready to be picked
fungee & pepper pot	the national dish of Antigua and Barbuda
fungee	a cooked paste made from cornmeal usually with okra
funk up	to repeatedly squeeze an unripen fruit
fuss	first

G

gad	God
galavant	to roam aimlessly
gallery	a covered front porch
ganga	marijuana, cannabis
garling	egret
garn way	gone away
garn	to leave

Antigua and Barbuda Dictionary

garrot	a term used by other Eastern Caribbean islanders to refer to a person from Antigua
gee	*to* give
georgie bungle	personal possession or belongings
giggie shit	diarrhea
gimme um	give it to me
ginger beer	a refreshing drink made from ginger root
git up	get up
give thanks	an expression of gratitude
goat water	a stew that is prepared using goat meat and a variety of herb, spices, and flour
goddie	godmother
gogo navel	an abnormal bulge that can be seen or felt at the belly button (umbilical hernia)
goo way fram yah	go away from here
goo way	to travel; get away
googlie eye	large eyes or bulging eyes
googlie marble	the largest marble in a marble game
goose	a metal iron with an internal reservoir where hot coal is placed to generate heat for ironing clothes
graba	guava
grada	a bulldozer
gramophone	an old type of record player
grass bakkle	broken pieces of glass bottle

grassberry	a tart berry with a high acidic content (gooseberry)
grawndy	grandmother; granny
green fig	green banana
grip	suitcase
gronut	peanut
groot up	scratches on the arms, knees, or legs resulting from a fall
grudgeful	a beetle that gives off a strong unpleasant odor when threatened or disturbed (stinkbug)
grung cart	a homemade cart constructed from odd pieces of wood and other materials
grung swell	when something is plentiful
grung	ground; floor; a vegetable garden
guava cheese	a thick sweet paste made from guava pulp (guava paste)
gundy	the claw of a crab or lobster
gut rain	the flow of water that occurs due to heavy rain in ditches, sidewalk, and road
gut	stomach
gutta	a long narrow ditch or trench
gwarn	go ahead; go on; be off; get out
gyal	a girl or young woman

H

hab	have

Antigua and Barbuda Dictionary

haffo	must or have to
hail up	to greet
hairbow	hair ribbon; hair clips
hairdo	hairstyle
halabalou	a tense situation or explosive brawl
ham roll	English pork sausage roll
hapenee	a unit of currency that equal to half of a penny
happaz	sneakers or tennis shoes
hard bound	to be constipated
hard enough	strong enough
hard head	a stubborn child or young person who does not listen
hard toan	an erection
hard up	to be sexually aroused; to be constipated
harden hole	an odd or unusual feature next to the ear resembling a hole
harden	a stubborn child who does not listen
hark	hawk
harmon	almond
harmoo	a cow
harrals	to give someone a hard time
hat	to hurt
haunted	a person who is bored or restless
head condom	a plastic shower cap
head master	the principal of a school
head tie	wraps used for covering the head
heap/hole heap	a large amount
hebby	heavy

hegging	refers to a person who whines and complain a lot
hellava	very large or gigantic
helt	health
heng sleep	to sleep for a long time
heng	to hang
highty tiety	a conceited person who looks down on others
hip and drop	a person who walks with a limp
hise	to lift up
hog mouth	a person who has a mouth that resembles a pig snout.
hoggish	to speak to a person in a rude harsh tone
holiday	vacation
hoosh	a command given for a dog to attack
horse spider	the Antiguan and Barbuda black tarantula
hot pepper	scotch bonnet or habanero pepper
hubble	a straight close-fitting skirt
husban	husband
hush	to stop talking; to shut up

I

ice box	refrigerator
ice water	drinking water made cold with pieces of ice or by being refrigerated
ignorance	to talk foolishness or nonsense

ignorant	one who is quick tempered
ile stove	a stove that operates with kerosene oil
in deh	in there
inna	in the
instral	intestine
intelli-dunce	an intelligent person who cannot fight the urge to use his or her intelligence for silliness and entertainment
interfere	to trouble
iony	a silver ball bearing that is used as a marble
irie	described something that is good or having self-respect
irish potato	white potato
iron band	a kind of traditional musical group in the folk culture of Antigua and Barbuda, characterized by using pieces of metal as musical instruments
iron bird	an airplane
isin	icing
it sweet me see	to take pleasure and comfort in another person's failure or misery
ital	organic natural wholesome foods eaten by Rastafarians

J

j'ouvert	the beginning of carnival celebration which involves a frenzy of dancing in

	the street accompanied by steel drum and brass bands
jabless	a character in Caribbean folklore. The legend says that she was born human but her deals with the devil made her become a demon
jack	an idiomatic expression – will you? I meant it
jack-a-lantan	a legendary spirit in the form of a small ball of fire or a strange looking light moving among trees at night luring a person to follow it into the distance
jah	Rastafarian name for former Ethiopian ruler Emperor Haile Selassie
jailbird	a derogatory term for a convicted criminal, especially one who's been in and out of jail several times.
jam	to poke
jammin	having a good time; to enjoy oneself at a party or festival
jampeepee	antlion; doodlebug
jap	to drop
jappaz	plain white spoon size dumplings made for soups and stews
jarpot	a clay earthen vessel that is used for storing water
jeck up	diseased root vegetables

jew	water in the form of droplets on plants due to condensation (dew)
jezebel	an ill-tempered vindictive woman
jhoint	a pool hall or bar
jive	to drive
John bull	a male masquerader dressed in crocus bag, dried banana leaves, mask, and two cow horn protruding from the head
join up	a style of penmanship (cursive) in which some characters are written joined together
joke sweet	to have a good laugh
jokie	a person who is funny, comical, or humorous
juey	fiddler crab
jumbee bead	the red and black seed of the climbing legume Abrus precatorius tree
jumbee soursop	a foul smelling and bitter tasting fruit. The leaves of the plant are sometimes used to treat a variety of health conditions (noni)
jumbee tree	the silk cotton tree known for its cotton like fibers
jumbee umbrella	edible and non-edible mushroom
jumbee	ghost or spirit of a dead person
jump up	to get up and dance
junk	drunk or intoxicated
just so	just like that

K

kakaroach	roach
kaka wheel	a naked thread spool
kang kang	a stiff garment worn under a dress or skirt
kasada	a starchy tuberous root of a tropical tree, used as food in tropical countries but requiring careful preparation to remove trace of cyanide from the flesh (cassava)
katchup	to share the living space of a friend or family member; to huddle or to sit closely to someone or something
kenip	an oval fruit that grows in bunches on trees up to 30 meters high (guinep)
kerchief	handkerchief
ketch	to catch
k-foot	knock knee
kimbo	to remove your hands from your hips
kinn	skin
kip woman/man	a married man or woman who is having an extra marital affair
kip up	a celebration (i.e. a wedding reception, birthday party)
kip	keep

kiss me libba	kiss my liver
kiss me rass	kiss my ass
knock about	to be used up
knock up	not to worry
knuckle	to cheat or to have an affair
kola stoppa	the cap from a sweet drinks or soda bottle
kong	to strike someone with a comb, brush, or other object
kracken	not feeling well; not doing well
kraney	a person who is very skinny
kudum	to strike a person using the elbow
kushu	cashew seed or nut
kushuma	cashew apple
kuzen	cousin

L

labba	to talk or to gossip
lack arf	to turn off
lack arn	to turn on
laff	laugh
lakka	like
lammie	a baby lamb
lamo shay	a jump rope game
lamp poas	an electrical pole
lang gut	said of someone who is able to consume large amounts of food
lang out	to stick out or to extend
lang	long; one who is notably tall

Antigua and Barbuda Dictionary

larn	learn
larnz	a bee sting
larry back	underwear made from flour bag or other fabric
larry	truck
lars lick	a person who strike or hit last
lars nite	last night
lars	last; loss
lashing	a beating
last lap	the last day of carnival when all bands descend on the streets and people play mas until dawn
latrine	an outhouse
lawd have mercy	an idiomatic expression - used during times of happiness or distress
leavins	leftover or uneaten food
ledda	leather; waist belt
lef yu poopa	leave your father; a request made to leave something alone
lef	to leave
leggo beast	a woman of loose morals; a prostitute
leggo	to let go
leh me lone	leave me alone
leh we go	let us go
lemme	let me
liard	a person who lies
lib	live
libba	liver

lick dung	to knock down
lick out	to knock out
licker	a long thin piece of metal that is used for cutting grass
lickerish	a person who is greedy
licks	a beating; to strike or to hit
likkle	little
lime	to hang out; to pastime
lint way	to melt away
liquid gold	100% proof rum
liss tongue	a speech defect; to speak with a lisp
lissen	listen
lizzy dog eye	a person who has a lazy eye
loco	train or locomotive
long eye	a person who is envious of someone else's possession; one who is greedy
long garlin time	long time ago
look deh	look there
look noh	an expression of annoyance
look yah	look here
loose	a female who is sexually indiscriminate
loot	to beg
love worm	the s-shaped matter that's excreted from a pimple
low	to act cheap; stingy; not giving
low-wait	to keep an eye on something or someone
lub	love
lutaz	a skin fungus

luvaz	window shutters with horizontal slats that are angled to admit light and air (louvers)

M

mackintosh	a waterproof bed cover made from rubberish fabric
mad	a person who is mentally ill or have mental health issues
mammie	mommy; mother
manchineel tree	a poisonous tree with leaves that blister the skin. The trees are usually found along the shoreline of beaches
manish	a boy acting like a grown man
man-john	tomboy
mannaz	manners; to show respect
marcie	slippery dense moss grass usually found around the edges and bottom of ponds and quarries
mark	to check or correct a student class work or assignment
markit	market
marnin	morning
marrid	married
martal	mortal; a living human being
marworm	is asked of someone who is chronically hungry

mas	a carnival that involves music, dancing, singing, drinking, and socializing
mash	to accidentally or intentionally step on someone's foot
mash dung	to destroy
mash up	to end a romantic relationship; to break up with a boyfriend or girlfriend, to end a marriage; to destroy
maskitta	mosquito
matta	matter; pus
mawga	a skinny malnourish looking person
maymay lippy	a nosey person
meddle	to get involve in someone business or affair
medsin	medication
mek arwe go	let us go
mek out	doing one's best
mek style	to show off
mek	make
mekine	any type of meats prepared with a meal
melee	gossip or rumors
melee around town	talk of the town
melee man	to be well informed about another person business
memba	remember; member
merasmie	sickly or unhealthy
me haffo	I must

Antigua and Barbuda Dictionary

me nah go	I am not going
me nah tek um	I am not taking it
me narm	I am not going to
me noh like um	I don't like it
me noh noh	I don't know
me noh quay	I don't care
me noh	I know
me yah	I'm here; I'm doing well
micase	to hurry up; make haste
micee bat	a flying bat
micee	mice
miggle	middle
min	was
mine	to watch over a baby or young child
mingo	Santo Domingo
miserable	a chronic complainer or an unhappy person
missa	mister
mo	more
mock money	fake money
mock yu may	to make a fool out of a person
moko jumbee	stilt dancers - typically seen during carnival
monee	money
mongrel	a dog that does not have a pedigree
moses boat	a very large ill-fitting shoes
mountain chicken	giant ditch frogs found on the island of Dominica and Montserrat
mouth briggle	dry saliva at the corners of the mouth
mouth organ	harmonica

move fram deh	move away from there
mugo	another word for twat or mug; a piece of a mug or the whole mug depending on the situation
mukky	muddy; murky
muma	mother
mumu	a foolish person
murda	an expression used during times of happiness or distress; murder
mussi	must be
mutton	meat from old sheep

N

naal/narl	not
nable tring	the dry remnant of a baby's umbilical cord
nable	navel; belly button
nack	to hit or strike
nah	not
naked rum	straight rum
nancie story	a folktale in the Caribbean with the trickster Anansi (a spider) as the lead character
narsie	nasty
nastiness	an expression of disgust
natty	knotted; a person with dreadlocks
nayba	neighbor
nayga house	people's home or house
nayga	people
neegle	dragon fly; needle

nenyam	food
neva	never
new yark	New York
nex	next
nitee	sleepwear
nize	noise
noh able	not able
noh ask me nuttin	don't ask me nothing
noh behave yah	to lack self-control or respect for self and others
noh gree	to be at odds with another person
noh nyam um	do not eat it
nonbaddy	no one; nobody
nort	zero
nose hole	nostril
nuff	a nosey or inquisitive person
nuttin	nothing
nyam broad	to eat good food
nyam	to eat
nyce	nice

O

o'lawd	an idiomatic expression – typically used during times of happiness or distress
obeah man	one who practice black magic as a profession
obeah	a collection of beliefs and spiritual practice associated with evil, luck, and healing

okro	okra
odda	other
old young	an old person who dresses and behaves younger than his or her age
ole	old
one tip and go	a generic game like cricket in which the batter must run once the bat strikes the ball
one twenty-one	best clothing
ongle	only
ooman	woman
ooyaiyai	an exaggerated response to something unpleasant
operation	surgery
out a vogue	out of fashion
out lardin	to be loud
outta	out of
ova	over
over stay	to stay illegally in a county beyond approve time
overseas	to travel abroad
own way	a defiant child or young person who does not listen

P

packin	a piece of vehicle tire
packin night	an annual event that once took place on November 5th characterized by bonfire and fireworks. The

	purpose was for people to burn their bad memories
pah	street; road
pampa laylay	expresses that something unpleasant is going to happen to someone who has done something wrong; to tell on someone
pampalam/pam	vagina
pan dem	on them
pan tap	on top
pan	on
pangcake	pancake
pani	an empty paint can or larger container used for carrying water
pankoot	an idiot or stupid person
pap	porridge
papa bird	Sir Vere Cornwall Bird Sr. – the first Prime Minister of Antigua and Barbuda
papa	father; grandfather
paper flower	a large claiming shrub that is used as hedge. The most common species of bougainvillea
parasol	umbrella
parch	to roast
parden	pardon
parson	pastor
parsa	pasture
party sweet	a lively party

pashan	to have a tantrum; one who is angry or upset
pat spoon	a large cooking or serving spoon
pattie	a flaky pastry pocket stuffed with meat, chicken, or saltfish
pear	avocado
peepee	to urinate
peerpa	paper
peesa	piece of
pem dog	to spit with intensity or vengeance at someone
penny hapenee	three cents
peppa	pepper
pepper pot	a dish made with a variety of green leafy vegetables, squash, fresh herbs, seasonings, hot pepper and different meats
puh poy	a torpedo oval or pear-shaped fruit (papaya)
pickcha	picture
pickanyegah	children
picking wilks	long pants that stop above the ankle
pickins	hog food – a mixture of discarded food, rotten fruits, fruit skin, vegetables, and vegetable skin
pickney	child
picky head	very short hair that does not grow
picky-picky	a person who is hard to please
piddle	to urinate
piggy	vagina

pile	hemorrhoid
pilla	pillow
pine	pineapple
pipe	a water tap that is placed at various locations for villagers to obtain water
pit	spit
pitatae pudding	a baked sweet desert made from grated sweet potato, grated coconut, flour, raisins, sugar and spices
plamplam dumplin	one who has a round flat face
play mas	to participate in a parade, float, or troop during carnival
playing big ooman	a young girl or child who behaves like an adult.
plentee	a lot
poas	to mail
poasman	postman or mailman
poe	chamber pot
pork	the vagina
pompa foot	a person who has one leg being larger than the other
pompa	oversize; hefty; very large
pompous	exhibiting self-importance
poop	to pass gas; to fart
poopa	father: papaya
poopoo	to defecate
poor boas	one who is boastful
poor house	a place where poor people live

poppy show	a person who looks ridiculous; a fool
porto reco	Puerto Rico
pram	a covered four-wheel baby carriage
prangrana	pomegranate
prapa	proper
pressure	high blood pressure; hypertension
pretty handsome	firefly; a good-looking man
provision	a combination of cooked or uncooked root vegetables, and green banana
pumpum fly	an annoying gnat
pumpum shorts	short pants that are tight enough that the imprints of the genitals are clearly visible
pumpum	vagina
puppy dog	a person who is a follower
pussy bubby	bantu knots - a hair style resembling the nipples of a domestic cat
pussy	a domestic cat
pussyclaat	a body part intended to be the target of a vicious brutal blow
put dung yu mooma	put down your mother
pwile fish	a child who is overindulged by his or her parents
pwile	spoil
pye assing	to play around or fool around

Q

quarrel	arguing or fighting

quart	twenty-five cents
quay/kay	care

R

raart	to tell someone off
rada	rather
rag up	to destroy
ragamuffin	dirty clothes; torn clothes
ragup 11 & tefin 12	a person who is dirty and unkept in appearance
rample	wrinkle
rass	ass; rear end; to beat
rassclaat	used as an expression of surprise, shock, or frustration
rasshole	a derogatory term for a person of ill repute
ratta	rat
raw back	Antigua & Barbuda Creole
rax	spit particle
raycan	herring that have been salted and smoked
rechile	with child; to be pregnant
redmem	a person who is extremely light in complexion
relish	types of meats served with a meal
renk	having a strong unpleasant urine smell
retch	to reach
revelling	having a great time

rice pap	a porridge made with cooked rice, milk, sugar and spices
rice pudden	a tubular sausage made with rice, animal blood, herbs, plenty seasonings and is stuffed into a cow or pig intestine. The sausage is then cooked until tender
riddim	the instrumental accompaniment of a song in Caribbean music, usually with a drum pattern and a prominent bassline
ride	to have sexual intercourse
rigglers	mosquito lava
ring neck chicken	a hen that has no feather around its neck
rishie	a fishy smell
road march	a musical composition hit song that is given an official title and is played often during carnival
roti	a traditional Indian bread eaten with different curried meats or vegetable
rounders	a game in which a softball is hit by hand and the player must run from base to base
row	fish eggs; caviar
rubba	eraser; condom
rubbaz	tennis shoes or sneakers
rubbish	garbage; trash; litter
ruction	a disturbance; confusion

rum shop	a small shop where men hangout to drink alcohol, conversate, play cards and other games
rummie	a person who drinks a lot of alcohol
rush	popular

S

safe	a cabinet made of wood and gauze and is used for storing food and other goods
saff	soft
salt	to be unlucky or to being in an unfortunate situation
saltbeef	beef cured in a liquid salt brine
saltfish	a fish dried and cured with salt (typically cod); vagina
santapee	centipede
sappy	over cooked food that is wet or mushy
sarbice	to recover from blows
sarch	search
sarda	an element (led) used to repair holes in enamel pots and pans
sarry	sorry
satday	Saturday
savier	savior
sax	socks
scaley	rough dry skin that resembles fish scale

scamp	a person who is not trustworthy
scampa	to scatter
scarce	something that's in short supply or hard to find
scatta	to disperse; to get away from a situation
scunt	the vagina; use as a derogatory curse word
scyance	a stuck-up or snobby female
sea bud	sea cucumber
sea needle	sea urchin
seasoned rice	a one pot rice dish that is well seasoned and contains a variety of fresh herbs, meats, vegetables, and peas
seben	seven
seed	testicles
seen	used to acknowledge what another person is saying (i.e. I understand; I agree)
sekkle	settle
sen croy	St. Croix
sen jan	St. John's
sen tamas	St. Thomas
sen	send
senna	an herbal tea laxative
sensemilla	marijuana; cannabis
seringle dingle	a person who is dirty and unkept in appearance

set up	cloudy sky indicating the possibility of rain; or to make an ugly facial expression by twisting up the face
shack-shack	a long brown pod that grows on the flamboyant tree
shad	a herring-like food fish of the genus Alosa and related genera that migrate from the sea to freshwater to spawn
shadduck	grapefruit
shaligo	blue crab
shap	shop
sharp	a man who is good at picking up women; well dressed
sha-sha	corn bread
she young-young	a person who cries easily or acts like a baby
shilling	a unit of currency used in some current and former British Commonwealth countries
shit mashers	plastic sandals
shoe counter	the back upper ridge of a shoe
shooda	should have
shoot hard labor	to work hard at physical labor
shu	a verbal command used to drive away chickens and roosters
shub	to push
shut	shirt
sicknin	a person who is annoying
sickum	a command given for a dog to attack

siddung	sit down
sinkle bible	aloe vera
sissa	sister
sizzers	scissors
skellingtan	skeleton
skin out	to expose the genital area by spreading the legs
skin teeth	to smile or grin
skylark	a person who plays around or play the fool
slabby	a person who is overweight and carries excessive body fat that giggles when they walk.
slack	lewd, indecent, or offensive behavior
slackness	inappropriate behaviors or action
slap-pale	a portable bedside pan used for urinating and defecating
slate	a personal hand-held chalk board
slewey	slippery
slice up	a sweet chunky coconut candy drop
slip	petticoat; undergarment
slippaz	slippers; flip flops
smaddy	somebody
smell high	a loud offensive body odor
snat pap	arrow root porridge
snat	nasal mucus
soca	a popular style of Caribbean music from Trinidad and Tobago.

solar verse	used to describe something that is completely out of this world
soldier crab	hermit crab
sometimeish	a moody person
sore foot fly	flies that are attracted to infected sores
soukuna	an old female vampire that sheds her human skin and flies at night as a ball of fire sucking the blood of her victims
sour tomuck	indigestion; acid reflux
soursop soup	a drink made from the juice of the soursop fruit
souse	boiled pig trotters or other meats served cold in a tasty seasoned sauce with lime, onion, garlic, minced hot pepper, cucumber and other spices
spar	friend
speak and spoke	to speak using correct grammar
speck	eye glasses
spitch	to dive into water
squeezy	dish-washing liquid
starlight	a hand-held slow burning firework
steelpan	a musical instrument originated in Trinidad. It is an acoustic percussion instrument made from steel stretched into a concave shape and attached to a hollow cylindrical resonator called a skirt

steups	a sucking noise made by pressing the tongue against the teeth to express annoyance or disapproval
sticking plaster	bandage
stinging nettle	a wild weedy plant that produce a stinging sensation upon contact
stinking toe	The fruit of the West Indian locust tree that has an edible dry pulp surrounding the seed
stone heap	a collection of stones used for drying, airing out, and bleaching white clothes
strap	a waist belt
straw	dried coconut branches that's used to make baskets, hats, or mats
subben	something
sucker	the undeveloped unsweetened part of a sugar cane
suck-suck	a homemade frozen pop treat made in a small transparent plastic bag
sugar cake	a sweet treat made with grated coconut, sugar and spices
sugar	diabetes mellitus
sums	addition
sundee	Sunday
sunshade	sun glasses
sussu sussu	gossip or indecent news about the private affairs of others
swaaty	fat or obese
sweet biscuit	sweet crackers or cookies

sweet drinks	carbonated soda
sweet eye	a wink or a flirtatious look
sweet ile	cooking oil
sweet talk	to flirt, charm, or entice
sweeties	candy

T

tack dung	to dress nicely or well dressed
take away	subtraction
tam	a large oval shaped hat that is used to cover dreadlocks
tambran	tamarind
tamp up	to stomp on
tampoose	teasing someone by repeatedly offering them something and taking it back
tan up	to stand up
tango	meat from old cattle or cow
tank	a large concrete structure used for catching, storing, and distributing water
tantie	aunt
tap lie	stop lying
tap yu chupitness	stop being silly
tap	stop
tark	talk
tarl	not at all
tart	a sweet pastry pocket filled with tropical fruit fillings
tase	taste

tata duhendeh	a mythical short man who lives in the bush, his feet are backward, and he has no thumb
tata	stutter
teacha	teacher
tear batty	pushing the rear end out and spreading the buttocks with both hands to insult another person
tear mouth	a person with a large wide mouth
tear pan	to stare or gaze at someone
teday	today
teely	penis
teet	teeth
tek	take
tekeen	to passed out, faint, or to get sick
tenite	tonight
tensel	chamber pot
ten-eye butterfly	monarch butterfly
tete	the pointed ends on a loaf of bread; the female breast
tie mouth	a strange sensation one gets in the mouth from biting into a sour or unripen fruit
tie tongue	having a stutter or speech impairment
tief way	to leave work without permission or without anyone knowing
tief	thief; to steal
tiff	stiff
tight	close relationship

tikle	title
tilet	toilet
ting	thing; girlfriend
tink	think; stink
titimus	tetanus
to bum	to beg for food; to hang around a person's house while they are cooking knowing that once the meal is prepared food will be offered.
to shy	the act of pretending to hit a person causing them to flinch or to protect their body
toan	penis
tomarra	tomorrow
tomuck	stomach
tongue lashing	to tell a person off
torch light	flashlight
tory	story
touches	to cry; to get offended easily
touris	tourist
trait	straight
tralala	confusion; scandal; argument
trang	strong
trash house	a house that is constructed of mud and dried coconut leaves as roofing
tree quarter drop shorts	Bermuda shorts
tree	the number 3
tring bang	a lot of children
trolang	to leave; to go away
troat	throat

trolley	a shopping cart
trus	to purchase something on credit
tump	to punch
tun rund	turn around
tun tick	a flat sturdy wooden stick used for cooking fungi
tun um arf	turn it off
tun um arn	turn it on
tun	to turn
tung	town; tongue
tunkoo	a steam roller
tuntun	vagina or female sexual organ
tuppence	the sum of two pennies
turkle berry	a sticky fruit like berry that is light pale to brown or even pink in color. The pulp in a ripe berry can be used as an alternative to paper glue
turkle	turtle
two-tongued	a deceitful person
tyaad	tired

U

ugly bad	real ugly
um	it
up and dung	to wander from place to place

V

vagabond	a person who is loud and display repulsive behaviors
valise	a small traveling bag or suitcase

veranda	a covered front porch
verlin	a West Indian name typically found on the island of Antigua and is given to guys who like to brag about their athletic skills which they don't have
vess	a close-fitting sleeveless top typically worn under a shirt or blouse
vex	to be upset
vice	voice
vim	cleaning powder
vum	to pass quickly

W

wadadli beer	the official beer of Antigua and Barbuda
wadadli	the original Amerindian name for Antigua and mean "our own"
waggi	hand-me-down clothing
wah gwaan?	What's going on?
wah mek?	why
wah yu know?	What do you know?
wah	what
walkbout	a person who is constantly on the move
walking stick	praying mantis
wall house	houses built of cement blocks and concrete
wantally	to purposely do something
wappie	an illegal gambling card game

wapsostatious	refer to something that is difficult to describe.
warbean	a promiscuous female
wark	walk
warrahee	buttocks or rear end
warri	a count and capture game that was brought to the West Indies from Ghana by slaves. Warri refers to the indentations carved into the game board. The game is played with 48 seeds, and the object of the game is to capture twenty-five counters.
wash arf	to take a partial bath
wash up	to clean/wash dirty dishes
wata	water
watch man	security guard
watch night	a night that involves a lot of mischief
water mouth	refers to babies who drool excessively
wedda peak	the hairline which makes a point at the middle of the forehead
wedda	weather
west Indian	someone from the Caribbean
wey	where
wheela	a bicycle rim and a long piece of metal wire with a curved hook end that guides the rim
whine	to dance in a sexually explicit or suggestive manner

who yu fah?	Who are your parents or people?
whoa	a command given to a donkey to stop
whofa	whose
whole heap	a large quantity; a lot; plenty
wi	first person plural pronoun meaning "we or us"
wicked	bad; evil
wid	with
wilks	whelk - a small aquatic snail often found attached to rocks along shoreline and beaches
willie monkey	an ugly person
winda	window
wink up	a dance that involve whining one's waist in a clockwise rotation to the beat of music
wishie washie	an indecisive person
wodd	to curse or to express feelings of displeasure to another person
wood slave	a small amphibian characterized by a lizard-like appearance -salamander
wooda	would have
wossara	worst
wotliss	worthless; lewd – refers to a person who lack domestic skills or one who carries themselves in a sleazy manner
wouldn	would not
wrang	wrong

wynn	wind

Y

yabba	a round cooking vessel made from clay
yah	here
yai	eye
yampee	mucus found at the corners of the eyes
yankee dollar	US dollars or currency
yap	to talk
yard fowl	free range chicken
yard	one's house or home
yu noh ezee	an idiomatic expression
yu wonderful	refers to a person who exhibits an over exaggerated emotional response to a situation
yute	youth; young people

Z

zaboca	avocado pear
zamy	a lesbian
zanana	pineapple
zed	the letter Z
zigum	used to tease a person who is engaging in behaviors that are risky
zinc	sheets of metal used for fencing or roofing; galvanize

zion cutlyss	a person who is not trustworthy or loyal to anyone
zoutupeg	an unpolished individual
zwag	a promiscuous female

Commonly used expressions and sayings

- **A little is better than nothing** – it's better to have that thing than to have nothing at all
- **A new broom sweeps clean, but an old broom knows the corners** – it is not always a good idea to get new everything, but experience is one of the best things to have
- **A pound of fret cannot pay an ounce of debt** – worrying does not solve or improve a bad situation
- **A rotten sheep will spoil the whole flock** – a single bad person can ruin everything around it
- **A watch pot never boils** – while waiting for something to happen, it feels like time is moving slower
- **A word better than a wink for a blind horse** – use the right motivation for each person
- **After laughter come tears** – after happiness comes sadness
- **All cassava got the same skin, but all cassava does not taste the same** – people may look alike, but they are unique in their own way
- **All fish bites, but shark always gets the blame** – those with a history of bad behavior are always the first ones accused
- **All skin teeth is not a laugh** – not everyone who smiles with you have good intention towards you
- **Alligator lay eggs, but he is not a fowl** – things are not always as they seem

Commonly used expressions and sayings

- **As you sow, so shall you reap** – if you did bad things in the past, you will get bad results in the future
- **Bad luck worse than obeah** – to be met with some type of misfortune is worse than an evil spell
- **Bad news travels fast** – when something negative happens, people learn of it quickly.
- **Bad things have no owner** – no one wants to take responsibility for a mistake or bad situation
- **Barking dogs seldom bites** – a person who often threatens rarely carries out his or her threats
- **Behind back have no ear** – does not translate
- **Better belly burst than good food waste** – it is better to over eat than to waste good food
- **Big house has big story** - does not translate
- **Black fowl can lay white egg** – what you perceive from how something appears might not be what it truly is
- **Blind man sees neighbors' faults** - does not translate
- **By you company you shall be known** – you are the company you keep
- **Carry go and bring come** – beware of people who bring you gossip about others, because they are equally likely to pass on gossip about you
- **Cat luck is not dog luck** – what one person might get away with may cause a problem for someone else

70

Commonly used expressions and sayings

- **Children and fools tell the truth** – children and fools say things without knowing or thinking what they mean, but often what they say is true
- **Clothes cover character** – the style and quality of peoples clothing is often an indication of their character
- **Cock mouth kill cock** – choose your words with care to avoid the risk of drawing unpleasant or unwanted attention to yourself
- **Cockroach have no right in a fowl's house** – it is dangerous to be in a place where you know your life is in danger
- **Come see me is one thing, come live with me is another** – no body truly knows another person until they have spent some time living together
- **Dirty water cool hot iron** - everything has its use
- **Don't cut off your nose to spite your face** – do not act to spite others that will harm you more than them
- **Don't hang your hat where your hand can't reach** – keep your goals within your abilities and means
- **Don't let sweet mouth fool you** – does not translate
- **Donkey got long ears, but don't like to hear his own story** – people don't like to take criticism
- **Empty bag can't stand** – a hungry person cannot work

Commonly used expressions and sayings

- **Empty vessel makes the most noise** – foolish people are the most talkative
- **Every cloud has a silver lining** – there is nothing bad that does not bring about something good
- **Every cook praises his own broth** – people tend to sing praise of their own work
- **Every day is fishing day, but every day is not catching day** – put forth effort every day but don't expect tangible rewards every day
- **Every dog is a lion in his own backyard** – people are always at their bravest or most self-assured when they are on their own home territory
- **Every pot has a cover** – there's someone for everyone
- **Every tub must stand on its own bottom** – people should be self-sufficient and not dependent on others financially or otherwise
- **Everyday bucket goes to well, one day the rope must cut** - if you repeatedly take the same risk, it will eventually end in disaster
- **Fisherman never smell his own basket** – people are oblivious to their own faults and flaws
- **Give a man enough rope and he will hang himself** – a person will bring about his own misfortune if given the opportunity
- **Give Jack his jacket** – give credit where credit is due
- **Good friend better than pocket money** – true friends are better than money

Commonly used expressions and sayings

- **Good fungee never meet good pepper pot** – good things rarely happen at the same time
- **Hand go hand come** – as you give, so shall you receive
- **Hunger make cat eat salt** – hard times force people to do strange things
- **If God spares life** – if I live to see another day
- **If you live in a glass house do not throw stones** – you should not complain about other people or criticize them unless you are perfect yourself
- **If you want to hear how the story goes, wait until quarrel come** - does not translate
- **Jumbee knows who to frighten at fore day morning** –bullies know exactly who they can abuse
- **Like a dog with a bone** – to refuse to stop talking or thinking about something
- **Little axe cut down big tree** – you don't have to be big to take on a big task
- **Monkey knows which tree to climb** – people know exactly who to manipulate and who to take advantage of
- **Monkey see monkey do** – people will do like others without thinking
- **Moon run till daylight catches him** – your action and misdeeds will eventually have consequences
- **Mouth open, story jump out** – when people talk too much

Commonly used expressions and sayings

- **Never trouble trouble, 'til trouble trouble you** – stay out of trouble, but be prepared in case you become troubled
- **One hand can't clap** – you must work with others to achieve a common goal
- **Only the wearer knows where the shoe pinches**
- **Pastor christen his child first** – everyone takes care of his own first
- **Plantain sucker follows the root** – children follow parents' example
- **Shut mouth catches no flies** – nobody can blame you for things you never said
- **Still waters run deep** – a quiet person may have much knowledge or deep feeling.
- **Tell the truth and shame the devil** – it is better to tell the truth even though there may be good reasons not to
- **The door swings both ways** – what you do to me, I can do to you
- **The enemy of my enemy is my friend** – those who dislike or oppose the same person or thing are bound to be friends or allies
- **The higher monkey climb, the more he shows his backside** – the more one shows off, the more one is vulnerable to ridicules and criticism
- **The road to hell is paved with good intention** – you many have good intentions, but if you do not put them into practice you will achieve bad results

Commonly used expressions and sayings

- **Time longer than twine** – time will right or avenge all wrongs
- **Two-man rat cannot live in the same hole** – whenever possible, it helps for everyone to have their own space
- **What the eye does not see, the heart does not grieve over** – remaining ignorant or uninformed about something means it will not upset, anger, or worry someone
- **What you can lock from a thief, you can't lock from a liar** – don't talk when your mouth is full of lies
- **When thief thieves from thief, God laugh** – God laughs at poetic justice
- **Where there's smoke, there's fire** – there's always some reason for a rumor
- **You borrow money and make enemy** – debt always come between friends and family

Antigua and Barbuda Dictionary

References

wiwords.com/sayings
pinterest.com
https://www.encyclopedia.com
www.idiomconnections.com/proverbs.htm

Printed in Poland
by Amazon Fulfillment
Poland Sp. z o.o., Wrocław